The Death Penalty for Teens

A Pro/Con Issue

Nancy Day

HOT
PRO/CON
ISSUES

Enslow Publishers, Inc.

40 Industrial Road   PO Box 38
Box 398   Aldershot
Berkeley Heights, NJ 07922   Hants GU12 6BP
USA   UK

http://www.enslow.com

Library of Congress Cataloging-in-Publication Data

Day, Nancy.
    The death penalty for teens : a pro/con issue / Nancy Day.
       p. cm. — (Hot pro/con issues)
    Includes bibliographical references and index.
    Summary: Examines both sides of the debate over whether teens under the age of eighteen should be sentenced to death for committing murder.
    ISBN 0-7660-1370-7
    1. Capital punishment—United States—Juvenile literature. 2. Juvenile justice, Administration of—United States—Juvenile literature. 3. Juvenile delinquents—United States—Juvenile literature. [1. Capital punishment. 2. Justice, Administration of. 3. Juvenile delinquency.] I. Title. II. Series.

HV8699.U5 D3 2000
364.66'0835'0973—dc21

                                      00-021971

Printed in the United States of America

10 9 8 7 6 5 4 3 2 1

To Our Readers:
All Internet addresses in this book were active and appropriate when we went to press. Any comments or suggestions can be sent by e-mail to Comments@enslow.com or to the address on the back cover.

Illustration Credits: Courtesy of the Communications Office of the California Department of Corrections, p 1; AP/Wide World Photos, pp. 6, 8, 16, 22, 26, 29, 32, 40, 46, 50.

Cover Illustration: Photograph provided by the Communications Office of the California Department of Corrections. Shown is the execution chamber with the lethal injection table at San Quentin Prison.

Contents

Chapter 1

Brief History of the Death Penalty

America was still under the British flag. George Washington would not be born for another one hundred years. It would be over one hundred fifty years before the United States Constitution was written. In that year of 1622, Daniel Frank was caught stealing. For his crime, he was sentenced to death. Frank became the first person to be executed in what would one day be the United States.[1]

The Death Penalty in United States History

Death penalty statistics were not kept properly until 1930. However, executions were carried out regularly. In the 1960s, people opposing the death penalty began to put pressure on government officials. As a result, a halt on executions began in 1967 even though the death penalty was still legal in forty states. Each state (as well as the federal government) had its own laws and ways of dealing with capital crimes (crimes punishable by death). From

*A*fter being convicted of murder, Gary Gilmore was executed by a firing squad in Utah on January 17, 1977. Gilmore's execution was the first in the United States in ten years.

1930 until 1967, there were 3,859 people executed in the United States.[2]

Then, in 1972, cases were brought before the U. S. Supreme Court to challenge whether the death penalty was legal under the United States Constitution. (The Constitution forbids "cruel and unusual punishment.") The Supreme Court justices ruled that the death penalty was cruel and unusual in the ways the states were using it. They said that the way decisions were being made about who would get the death penalty was unfair. In particular, they said that blacks were being given the death sentence more often than whites. After this ruling, there could be no executions in the United States. More than six hundred inmates had their death sentences reduced to life in prison. But within a few years, states changed their laws to establish death penalty guidelines that would be acceptable to the Court. The death penalty was reinstated, or put back into practice.

Executions began again in 1977 with a blast of gunfire. Gary Gilmore, a convicted murderer, was executed by a firing squad on January 17, 1977. It was the first execution in the United States in ten years. For the next seven years, there were few

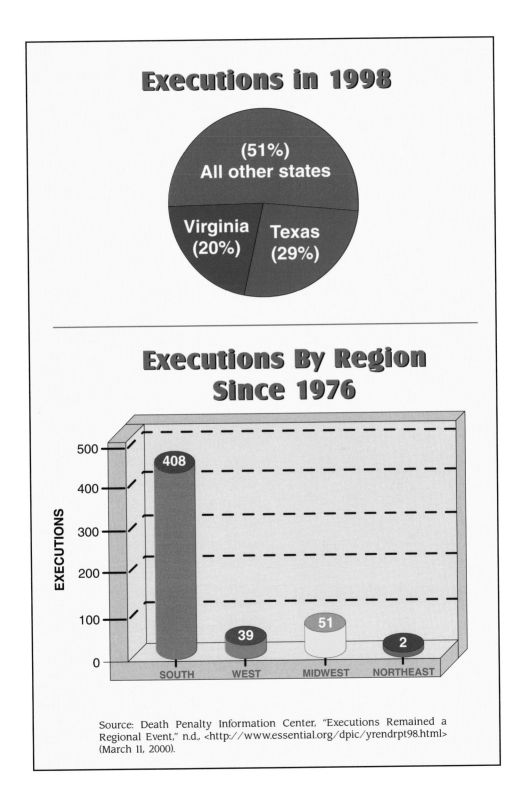

Executions in 1998

(51%)
All other states

Virginia
(20%)

Texas
(29%)

Executions By Region
Since 1976

EXECUTIONS

500	
400	
300	
200	
100	
0	

408

SOUTH

39
WEST

51
MIDWEST

2
NORTHEAST

Source: Death Penalty Information Center, "Executions Remained a
Regional Event," n.d., <http://www.essential.org/dpic/yrendrpt98.html>
(March 11, 2000).

executions. But in the mid-1980s, due in part to pressure to "get tough on crime," states began performing more executions. In 1984, the number of executions jumped to twenty-one. By 1999, there were ninety-eight executions in a single year.

From the time the death penalty was reinstated in 1976 until January of 2000, there were 613 executions in the United States. The practice is more common in the South, where 495 of the executions took place. Of these, 281 were in just two states: Texas and Virginia.[3]

The most common forms of execution are lethal injection, electrocution, and the gas chamber.

During lethal injection, the drugs that stop the heart and other body functions are pumped into the body through the veins. Electrocution is sending jolts of electricity through a person's body. A gas chamber is a sealed room into which poisonous gases are released. The prisoner dies from breathing in the poisonous gases. From 1976 to January 2000, 445 people have been executed by lethal injection, 145 by electrocution, 11 by the gas chamber, 3 by hanging, and 2 by firing squad.[4]

*T*he electric chair is the second most common form of execution. This chair was prepared by the Southern Ohio Correctional Facility in 1997 for the state's first execution since 1963.

The total number of people on death row has

risen dramatically since the mid-1970s. In 1974, there were 244 people awaiting execution. By 1999, the number had risen to 3,625.[5] The ninety-eight executions that took place in 1999 were the most for any year since the death penalty was made legal again in 1976.

The Death Penalty in World History

The death penalty has been used by nearly every culture since ancient times. In recent history, the trend has been for countries to find other ways to deal with criminals.

By December 1999, seventy countries had abolished (gotten rid of) the death penalty for all crimes. Thirteen countries had abolished it for all but unusual cases, such as war crimes. Twenty-three countries had abolished it in practice (They have not executed anyone for at least ten years even though they have a death penalty.) However, capital punishment remains a common practice in a number of countries, with only a few countries making up the majority of executions worldwide.

Ninety countries use the death penalty. However, the number that actually execute people in a given year is quite small. According to Amnesty International, an organization that works to protect human rights, during 1998 there were at least 1,625 prisoners executed in thirty-seven countries. (The exact number cannot be known.) The countries with the largest numbers of executions were China (1,067), Congo (100), United States (68), and Iran (66).[6]

Pros and Cons of the Death Penalty

The debate over the death penalty draws strong opinions from both sides. Some people think the death penalty is cruel. Other people say that it is the only way to reduce crime.

Is the death penalty morally acceptable? For many people, the death penalty is a means of revenge. Someone who has killed, they say, has lost the right to live. The saying "an eye for an eye and a tooth for a tooth" is used to support this view. However, many religious groups oppose the death penalty because of moral reasons. In 1999, the United States Catholic Conference of Bishops issued a statement that said,

> We cannot overcome crime by simply executing criminals, nor can we restore the lives of the innocent by ending the lives of those convicted of

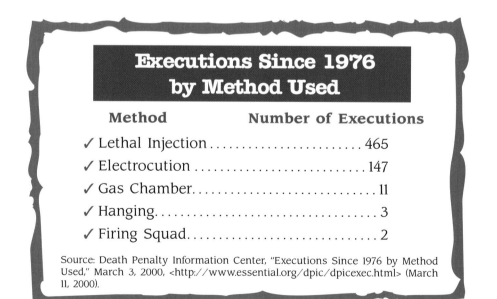

Executions Since 1976 by Method Used

Method	Number of Executions
✓ Lethal Injection	465
✓ Electrocution	147
✓ Gas Chamber	11
✓ Hanging	3
✓ Firing Squad	2

Source: Death Penalty Information Center, "Executions Since 1976 by Method Used," March 3, 2000, <http://www.essential.org/dpic/dpicexec.html> (March 11, 2000).

their murders. The death penalty offers the tragic illusion that we can defend life by taking life.[7]

Death penalty supporters say that victims and their families deserve justice. Although nothing will bring back a murdered loved one, supporters say that seeing the person responsible die for their crime helps families deal with their feelings of anger and powerlessness.

People who oppose the death penalty think that the taking of a life is never right, whether it is by an individual or by the government. They feel that no matter what someone has done, that person should have a right to life and a chance to change.

Some say having the government as executioner makes violence seem an acceptable way to deal with problems and may actually encourage more violence. They argue that killing people makes the government a murderer. Death penalty supporters point out that nations have no problem with killing people during war to protect their countries from outside dangers. Capital punishment, they say, is no different. It is a nation's way of protecting its citizens from dangerous criminals.

Is the death penalty economical? The costs involved in trying, processing, and either executing or imprisoning criminals for life are extremely high. Death penalty supporters say that executing a criminal is cheaper than keeping inmates in prison for their lifetimes. Those opposed say that when all the costs are added, life imprisonment is actually cheaper. They point to the expenses of additional trial time and the salaries of government lawyers who must put in extra work to prepare for death penalty cases. Opponents also point to the high cost of keeping a prisoner on death row for the many years it usually takes to go through all the appeals (requests that a case be reviewed).

Costs could be reduced by limiting the inmate's right to appeal. Appeals, which are usually based on claims that the original trial was not fair, take time because each appeal must be evaluated and can result in an additional trial. However, reducing the number of appeals might mean that people who did not get fair trial or were innocent of the crime might be executed. (Nearly half of the death penalty cases reviewed at the federal level have been reversed.)

Does the death penalty reduce crime? Supporters of the death penalty say that it reduces crime by scaring people who might commit crimes. Critics point to studies showing that states that have brought back the death penalty after abolishing it have not seen a drop in the murder rate. In addition, states that have the death penalty do not have lower murder rates than those that do not. In a 1995 national survey, police chiefs ranked the death penalty as the least effective means of controlling crime.[8]

Death penalty supporters say that comparing states is misleading because many of the states with death penalties are states that have always had higher crime rates. They say that national crime statistics show that the murder rate went down during years when there were many executions. However, the murder rate rose during the period when the death penalty was banned. To those who want to get rid of the death penalty because it is not a good deterrent, death penalty supporters say that it would be just as silly to get rid of prisons, since they do not seem to stop crime either.

One reason, some say, that executions are not an

effective way to reduce crime is because they are not performed quickly and consistently. If all convicted murderers were executed immediately, few would murder, they argue. But the chance that a murderer will be caught, tried in court, given the death penalty, and then executed is quite small. While there are thousands of murders a year, less than a hundred murderers are executed annually.

Critics say that the death penalty does not prevent murders because most killings occur in the heat of the moment or under the influence of drugs or alcohol. Murderers seldom stop to think about the consequences of their actions. Death penalty supporters say that the one certain thing is that if murderers are executed, those particular criminals will never murder again.

Are innocent people being executed? Death penalty critics say that the risk of killing an innocent person is too great. Mistakes can happen with any system, but once a person is executed it is too late to apologize. Between 1973 and 1999, eighty-four people were freed from death row and declared innocent. Some were freed only minutes before they were to be executed. That means one death row inmate has been released for every seven who have been executed.[9]

Unfortunately, not all innocent prisoners are as lucky. Within the last century, at least twenty-five people who were executed were later found innocent. Justice Moses Harrison II of the Illinois State Supreme Court said,

> Despite the courts' efforts to fashion [create] a death penalty scheme [plan] that is just, fair, and reliable, the system is not working. Innocent people are being sentenced to death . . . It is no answer to say that we are doing the best we can.

If this is the best our state can do, we have no business sending people to their deaths.[10]

Death penalty supporters say that no system is perfect. They point out that appeals are part of the process. And if prisoners are later found innocent, say supporters, that just shows that the system is working. They disagree with some of the cases in which supposedly innocent people were executed, saying that in some cases, evidence exists that the inmates were in fact guilty.

Modern technology such as DNA analysis may help decrease the chances of an innocent person being found guilty, by providing a way to determine guilt scientifically. Regardless, the need to protect society as a whole, say death penalty supporters, is more important than worrying about an occasional mistake.

Does the death penalty discriminate? More than half of the prisoners executed between 1930 and 1996 were African American. A study taken in Philadelphia showed that black defendants were four times more likely to receive the death penalty than members of any other ethnic or racial group. The report also noted that 98 percent of United States chief district attorneys (the people who decide whether to seek the death penalty) are white.[11]

Black offenders have been routinely executed for crimes such as rape that were not considered capital crimes for whites. Between 1930 and 1976 (the last year that the death penalty was used for the crime of rape), 455 men were executed for rape. Of these, 405 were African American.[12]

The race of the victim also seems to matter. Black men are particularly likely to be given the

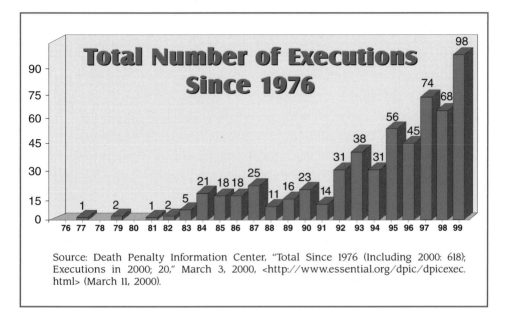

Source: Death Penalty Information Center, "Total Since 1976 (Including 2000: 618); Executions in 2000; 20," March 3, 2000, <http://www.essential.org/dpic/dpicexec. html> (March 11, 2000).

death sentence for crimes when the victim is white. Less than half of all murders involve white victims. Yet 82 percent of the prisoners executed since 1976 were convicted of murdering a white person. These statistics cause critics to say that the death penalty is discriminatory. United States Supreme Court Justice Harry Blackmun said, "Even under the most sophisticated death penalty statutes, race continues to play a major role in determining who shall live and who shall die."[13]

Some say that the death penalty also treats those with mental disabilities unfairly. People with limited mental capability may behave in ways that make them more likely to be arrested, wrongly convicted, and harshly sentenced, say critics. As recently as 1998, two mentally impaired men were executed in the United States.

The death penalty also seems to discriminate

against men. Although women make up one in every eight murder arrests, they account for only one in fifty death sentences. Actual executions of women are rare. The two women executed in 1998 were the first in nearly fourteen years.

Death penalty supporters say that if the death penalty discriminates, it is only because judges and juries do not have to give the death sentence in every case. If the death penalty was always given for certain crimes, there could be no discrimination.

Is the death penalty cruel? People who want to abolish the death penalty say it is cruel. In particular, they note the number of executions that did not go smoothly. The twenty-four cases they cite include the execution of John Evans in Alabama's electric chair in 1983. The execution lasted fourteen minutes. After the first jolt, smoke and sparks came out from under the hood covering Evans's head. Doctors found a heartbeat, so another jolt was given. This produced more smoke and burning, yet Evans was still alive. A third jolt finally killed Evans, leaving his body charred and smoldering. In 1997, Scott Carpenter endured eighteen violent

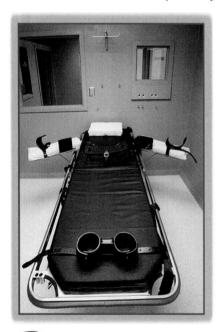

*D*eath penalty supporters say that lethal injection is the most humane form of execution. Prisoners of Oregon State Penitentiary who are sentenced to death are strapped to this gurney in the prison's execution chamber.

convulsions during the ten minutes it took him to die by lethal injection in Oklahoma.[14]

Death penalty supporters say that execution, particularly by lethal injection, is humane. Far more cruel, supporters say, is to make prisoners spend their entire lives behind bars. Besides, say supporters, why should people who have committed cruel acts be treated kindly? Where was the concern for humane treatment, they ask, when the offenders' victims were being brutally murdered?

Public Opinion

Polls generally show that most people support the death penalty. However, the support drops when alternative sentences are offered. A 2000 national survey by ABCNEWS.com showed that 64 percent of the public surveyed approved of the death penalty. But when life imprisonment without possibility of parole was offered as an option, support dropped to 48 percent. In general, public support for the death penalty seems to be slipping. A similar poll in 1996 showed 77 percent favoring the death penalty.[15]

Public opinion on the death penalty for juvenile offenders (people who committed their crimes when they were under the age of eighteen) varies. A number of organizations, including the American Bar Association (a professional organization for lawyers), oppose the death penalty for juveniles.

Some people think that the background of the juvenile offender is an important consideration. Research published in 1998 showed that of the fourteen juveniles on death row who had been examined for the study, all had suffered serious head injuries as children and all had serious psychological problems. Twelve of the fourteen had suffered serious physical abuse and five had been sexually abused as children.[16] The research also found many cases of alcohol and drug abuse and mental illness in the offenders' families. In addition, the researchers found that few of these details had come out in the prisoners' trials, even though they qualified as mitigating circumstances (factors that might have influenced the sentencing).

Critics call this "the abuse excuse" and say many people with troubled childhoods have made successes of their lives and not turned to crime. They say that allowing offenders to avoid responsibility is unfair to the victims and excuses criminal behavior.

Chapter 2

Executing Teens

Thomas Graunger of Plymouth Colony, Massachusetts, was the first known juvenile offender executed in America. Graunger was hanged in 1642 at the age of sixteen. He may have been the first but he was not the last. Nor was he the youngest. In 1944, George Stinney was executed in South Carolina. He was fourteen years old and so small that authorities had trouble fitting him in the electric chair. Although no children under the age of eighteen have been executed in the United States in recent years, states continue to execute inmates for crimes committed as juveniles.

Teens Executed in the United States

When the colonists came to America, they set up a legal system similar to the one they had in England. Under that system, people fourteen or older were considered responsible for their actions and therefore tried and punished as adults. This included being given the death penalty. Even children as young as seven could be tried and

Executions of Juvenile Offenders

January 1, 1973, through present

Name	Date of Execution	Place of Execution	Race	Age at Crime	Age at Execution
Charles Rumbaugh	9/11/85	Texas	White	17	28
J. Terry Roach	1/10/86	South Carolina	White	17	25
Jay Pinkerton	5/15/86	Texas	White	17	24
Dalton Prejean	5/18/90	Louisiana	Black	17	30
Johnny Garrett	2/11/92	Texas	White	17	28
Curtis Harris	7/1/93	Texas	Black	17	31
Frederick Lashley	7/28/93	Missouri	Black	17	29
Ruben Cantu	8/24/93	Texas	Latino	17	26
Chris Burger	12/7/93	Georgia	White	17	33
Joseph Cannon	4/22/98	Texas	White	17	38
Robert Carter	5/18/98	Texas	Black	17	34
Dwayne Allen Wright	10/14/98	Virginia	Black	17	24
Sean Sellers	2/4/99	Oklahoma	White	16	29
Douglas Christopher Thomas	1/10/00	Virginia	White	17	26
Steven Roach	1/13/00	Virginia	White	17	23
Glen McGinnis	1/25/00	Texas	Black	17	27

Source: Death Penalty Information Center, "Executions of Juvenile Offenders," n.d., <http://www.essential.org/dpic/juvexec.html> (March 11, 2000).

executed for violent acts against people or property. In New England, an eight-year-old was hanged for burning a barn.

In 1899, a separate court system for juveniles was created. The idea was to set up a way to rehabilitate (return to society) young offenders rather than simply punish them. The juvenile justice system allowed judges to sentence youth offenders to probation (a period of close supervision), rehabilitation programs (programs designed to teach proper behavior), or imprisonment in juvenile detention facilities (jail-like institutions for kids). Nevertheless, courts continued to give the death penalty—regardless of the offender's age.

At least 286 juvenile offenders have been executed in the United States. Nearly two hundred have been executed since 1900. Twelve of the fifteen thousand recorded executions in the United States were offenders who were under the age of fourteen at the time of the crime.[1]

Due to the years it takes to process appeals in the United States, juvenile offenders are in their twenties or even thirties by the time the executions take place. Nevertheless, between 1990 and January 2000, the United States executed more juvenile offenders (eleven) than the rest of the world combined (nine). Of the five executions of juvenile offenders between 1997 and January 2000, all took place in the United States.[2] According to Amnesty International, the United States probably has more juvenile offenders on death row than any other country. In January 2000, there were seventy death row inmates who were sentenced as juveniles.

As with adult offenders, the highest number of executions of juvenile offenders occurs in the South. Texas and Florida have imposed twice as many juvenile death sentences as any other state. Three of the four cases involving female juveniles were in Mississippi, Alabama, and Georgia.

In 1998, three juvenile offenders were executed in the United States, despite protests from national and international human rights leaders. These were the first executions for crimes committed by

*A*t sixteen, Sean Sellers (left) was a satanist who had murdered three people. Thirteen years later, a changed Sellars (bottom, center) appealed for leniency before the Oklahoma Clemency Board. Even the American Bar Association protested his death sentence. However, Sellers was executed on February 4, 1999. He became the first person to be executed in the United States in forty years for a crime committed at the age of sixteen.

offenders under the age of eighteen since 1993. In 1999, for the first time in forty years, an offender was executed in the United States for a crime he committed at the age of sixteen. Sean Sellers had been convicted of killing his mother and stepfather. At an earlier time, he had also killed a shop clerk. At the time of his execution, Sean Sellers was twenty-nine. The American Bar Association and the United States High Commissioner for Human Rights were among those who spoke out against the Sellers execution.[3] Nevertheless, he was put to death. In 2000, Steven Roach became the youngest person (at the time of execution) to be put to death since 1976. He was twenty-three and was executed in Virginia for shooting a seventy-year-old woman, a crime committed when he was seventeen.

Worldwide Executions of Teens

In the United States, teen offenders are in their twenties or even thirties by the time the appeals run out and executions take place. In other parts of the world, this is not always the case. Although it is difficult to tell exactly how many executions of juvenile offenders take place internationally, Amnesty International has attempted to document them. From 1985 to 1995, the organization has counted at least twenty executions of people who were under age eighteen. One notable case is that of Nasser Munir Nasser al Okirbi, who was convicted of robbery and murder in Yemen and was hanged on July 21, 1993. He was thirteen years old.[4]

There are fifty children on death row in Pakistan. Mohammad Saleem, fourteen, was arrested in June 1998. He was accused of being involved with the murder of three police officers in the alley where he lives. He was sentenced to death by a military court. He was later found innocent due to a lack of evidence. Four months later, he was rearrested and retried on the same charges, despite the fact that this practice violates international law as well as Pakistan's own constitution.[5]

Dead Teen Walking—Juveniles on Death Row

Joseph Hudgins is a teen on death row. When he was seventeen, he and a friend, Terry Cheek, stole an Orkin pest control truck one night for a joyride. South Carolina deputy Christopher Lee Taylor stopped the truck after spotting a hose dragging behind the truck. One of the boys shot Taylor in the face, killing him. Hudgins confessed to the killing. The murder weapon was found in his home. He later said Cheek had committed the murder. However, Hudgins had agreed to take the blame because he was under eighteen and mistakenly thought he would get let off easier than Cheek would. Cheek pleaded guilty to accessory to murder (helping with the crime) in return for never being tried for the murder itself. Although Hudgins says Cheek was the one who fired the shot, Hudgins is the one who ended up on death row.[6]

Efrain Perez and Raul Villarreal are on death row in Texas. They were both seventeen when, as part of a gang activity, they and some friends drank and fought in a field one night. When Jennifer Ertman, fourteen, and Elizabeth Pena, sixteen, took a shortcut across the field, the six boys raped and killed the girls. Five of the offenders got the death penalty. The sixth, who was fifteen, got forty years in prison.[7]

These are just three of the seventy people on

death row for crimes they committed as teenagers. Juvenile offenders account for about 2 percent of all death row inmates. The number of teen offenders on death row has more than doubled since 1983.[8]

Current Status of Teens and the Death Penalty

Violent crimes committed by extremely young offenders have led some people to feel that the age for execution should be lowered. Former Governor Pete Wilson of California has suggested that fourteen-year-olds should be eligible for the death penalty. The governor's spokesperson said that gangs in California often use young members for killings because they know they will not be eligible for capital punishment. Lowering the age for the death penalty might stop this practice.

A rash of school shootings raised the issue again. What does society do with a fourteen-year-old who kills three students during a prayer meeting at a West Paducah, Kentucky, high school? What should be done with a sixteen-year-old in Pearl, Mississippi, who kills his mother, then goes to school and opens fire, killing three and wounding seven? What about a fifteen-year-old in Springfield, Oregon, who kills both his parents, then goes to school and shoots twenty-four students, killing two? Whenever events such as these occur, there is plenty of fault to go around: access to guns, failure to provide counseling, violence in the media, abusive parents or peers. Solutions are tougher. Are these offenders mentally ill children in desperate need of help? Criminals who should be severely punished? Vicious animals that should be killed?

In an attempt to deal with the problem, the

*W*earing a protective vest, Luke Woodham, age sixteen, is led from a Pearl, Mississippi, courtroom on October 2, 1997. He was accused of killing his mother before going on a shooting rampage at his high school.

United States Congress had considered passing the Violent and Repeat Juvenile Offender Accountability and Rehabilitation Act of 1999. The law would provide a billion dollars in federal money for crime prevention and to toughen prosecution of juvenile crimes. It would allow courts to try juveniles age fourteen or older as adults for violent crimes or serious drug offenses. It would also require courts to consider the offender's criminal record when sentencing a juvenile offender as an adult. By the beginning of 2000, Congress had not been able to agree on the bill and passage seemed unlikely.

Chapter 3

Arguments for the Death Penalty for Teens

People who support using the death penalty for juvenile offenders say that a person old enough to kill another human being is old enough to suffer the consequences. They point to the fact that crimes committed by children seem to be getting more violent. They believe that victims as well as society deserve to see criminals pay for their crimes, regardless of their age. The death penalty, according to its supporters, is a less expensive and more effective way to deal with young murderers than rehabilitation programs that may or may not work.

Juvenile Crime Is Out of Control

In the mid-1970s, Americans decided to crack down on juvenile crime. States began to lock up teen criminals and turn from a system that was focused on rehabilitation to one based on punishment. From 1978 to 1988, the juvenile crime rate dropped 19 percent, while the lockup rate increased 50 percent.[1]

In the mid-1980s, murders by fourteen- to twenty-four-year-olds began to rise dramatically. The increase was particularly noticeable for the fourteen- to seventeen-year-old age group. Since 1993, the rates have dropped significantly but are still above the rates prior to 1980.[2] Some people say that recent violent crimes involving children show that predictions that juvenile crime would get worse were right. In 1995, James Fox, dean of the Criminology Department at Northeastern University said: "There is a tremendous crime wave coming in the next 10 years." He predicted that the criminals would be "ruthless" children in their early and mid-teens. "We have seen a radical change in the nature of violence," he said. "Murderers are getting younger and younger."[3]

Teens can rack up a long list of charges without ever serving jail time. When four boys, all under the age of seventeen, killed a British tourist in a bungled robbery in Florida, one boy was found to have a record of fifty-six arrests. "Juveniles have learned a confrontation with the system is nothing to be feared whatsoever," says Paul McNulty of the First Freedom Coalition, a group that favors stiff punishments for juvenile offenders.[4]

Death penalty supporters say that the death penalty would get juvenile offenders to take the justice system seriously. If teen criminals knew that a murder conviction meant death, supporters say, the young offenders would think twice before committing the crime.

Age Is No Excuse for Violent Crimes

When the fire alarm rang at the Westside Middle School in Jonesboro, Arkansas, the students obediently began to file out. Suddenly, they were fired on as if they were targets at a shooting gallery. Four students and a teacher were killed. Ten others were injured. The police arrested Mitchell Johnson, age thirteen, and Andrew Golden, age eleven.

To the people who lost family members in the incident, it did not matter that the killers were children. Their loved ones were still dead. But what should be done with the killers? As *Time* magazine asked in the headline of an article on the incident, "What Is Justice for a Sixth-Grade Killer?" A man quoted in the story spoke for many: "I don't care how old they are; if they kill somebody, they ought to die. I don't care if they're five years old."[5]

As it turned out, in Arkansas, children under the

*M*iddle-school students grieved at a memorial service on March 31, 1998, for the victims of the Jonesboro, Arkansas, school shooting.

age of fourteen cannot be tried as adults. They are generally only imprisoned until the age of eighteen. Many people were angry that the boys would be locked up for less than ten years after committing multiple murders.

Death penalty supporters say that anyone old enough to murder is old enough to pay the penalty, even if that penalty is death. Miriam Shehane, president of Victims of Crime and Leniency (VOCAL), says, "If someone does adult crime, they are acting as adults, and they have to take responsibility."[6] Shehane thinks that the death penalty should be used not only for offenders with long histories of

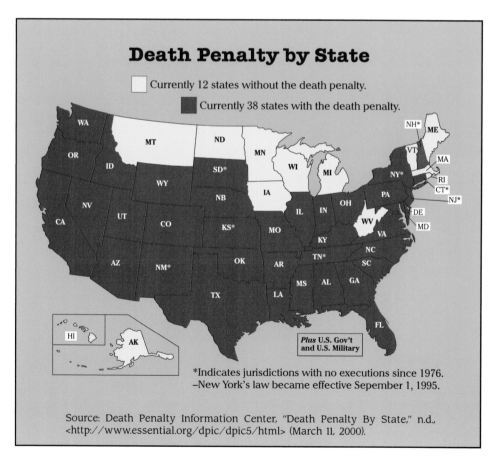

Death Penalty by State

☐ Currently 12 states without the death penalty.

■ Currently 38 states with the death penalty.

*Indicates jurisdictions with no executions since 1976.
–New York's law became effective Sepember 1, 1995.

Source: Death Penalty Information Center, "Death Penalty By State," n.d., <http://www.essential.org/dpic/dpic5/html> (March 11, 2000).

criminal behavior and violence but for those who commit a single severe crime.

Victims and Society Deserve Justice

At age thirteen, Craig Price stabbed a neighbor fifty-eight times. Two years later, he murdered three more people. Yet, because he was only fifteen years old, he was convicted and imprisoned as a juvenile. He was scheduled to be released at the age of twenty-one. Kevin Collins, a police captain who campaigned to stop Price's release, said "When this guy gets out, he'll have no criminal record whatso-ever. He can get a job at a day-care center or driving a school bus. He'll even be able to buy a gun."[7]

Should such a person be released after only six years? Many people believe that letting kids off easy for violent crimes does not serve society, the victims and their families, or even the offenders themselves.

Sometimes, the victim's family members are allowed to make victim impact statements to the jury to explain how the crime has affected them. Tom Morris, whose adult daughter Leanne Coryell was murdered, argued for the death penalty in his statement to jurors during the trial of Raymond Lamar Johnston. Johnston was convicted of driving Coryell to a vacant area behind a church and then beating her with a belt, raping, robbing, and strangling her. Morris told jurors: "I seriously doubt if any of the family will ever recover from the shock of the knock on the door in the early morning hours of Aug. 20, 1997 [when they learned of the murder]."[8]

Christina Wolfe was twelve when she was strangled. Randy Boddie, a close family friend who had known Christie her whole life, feels some comfort in

the fact that the murderer got the death penalty but wonders whether the execution will actually take place. "He is allowed appeal after appeal, which is far more 'chances' than Christie was allowed," Boddie says. He thinks that some families need to be able to see the murderer executed. It is their right, he believes, because it allows them to see justice done and get on with their lives.[9]

*D*eath penalty supporters say that anyone old enough to murder is old enough to pay the penalty. Fifteen-year-old Andrew Wurst is shown here attending a hearing to decide whether he will stand trial as a juvenile or as an adult for the 1998 murder of a middle-school teacher. It was later decided that Wurst would be tried as an adult.

Imprisonment Is Expensive, Rehabilitation Impossible

The kinds of problems that breed teen killers are complex and may be impossible to solve anytime soon. Long-term solutions such as cleaning up neighborhoods, solving the drug problem, ending abuse, and providing job opportunities will not protect society from teen killers today.

When teenage killers are convicted and put in prison for life, society must pay to feed and house them for fifty, sixty, seventy, or more years. Death penalty supporters say this is too much to ask. If these offenders will never be productive members

Minimum Age for Death Penalty by State		
Age Eighteen	**Age Seventeen**	**Age Sixteen**
California	Florida	Alabama
Colorado	Georgia	Arizona
Connecticut	New Hampshire	Arkansas
Illinois	North Carolina	Delaware
Kansas	Texas	Idaho
Maryland	**Total: 5 states**	Indiana
Montana		Kentucky
Nebraska		Louisiana
New Jersey		Mississippi
New Mexico		Missouri
New York		Nevada
Ohio		Oklahoma
Oregon		Pennsylvania
Tennessee		South Carolina
Washington		South Dakota
Federal government		Utah
Total: 15 states and federal		Virginia
		Wyoming
		Total: 18 states

Source: Information by Victor Streib, "The Juvenile Death Penalty Today: Death Sentences and Executions for Juvenile Crimes January 1973-June 1999," January 21, 2000, <http://www.essential.org/dpic/juvagelim.html> (March 11, 2000).

of society, they ask, why keep them alive for decades?

Some juvenile offenders have grown up being abused, taking drugs, and committing crimes. They may have histories of torturing animals, setting fires, and terrorizing the people around them. They have little understanding or concern about how their actions hurt others. What are the chances of rehabilitating such a person? Death penalty supporters say that the chances are slim to none.

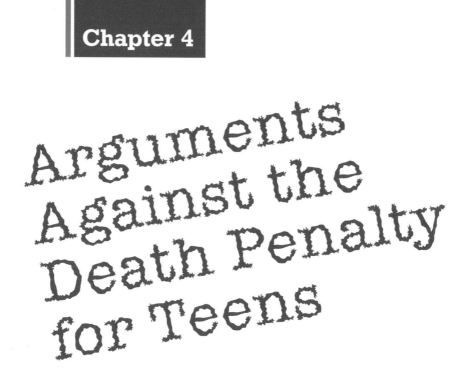

Chapter 4

Arguments Against the Death Penalty for Teens

Some people oppose the death penalty in all cases. Others believe that capital punishment has a place in society but argue that its use for juvenile offenders is wrong. They say that not only does the death penalty not reduce juvenile crime, but it is uncivilized, biased, and morally wrong. They believe that children who commit even the most violent crimes should have a chance to turn their lives around.

Civilized Countries Do Not Execute Children

The Geneva Conventions, a series of international treaties designed to ensure humane treatment for both soldiers and civilians during times of war, provide basic guidelines for civilized behavior. The 1949 convention contained the statement that "the death penalty may not be pronounced on a protected person who was under eighteen years of age at the time of the offense."[1] In other words, according to the Geneva convention, executing people who were under age eighteen at the time of the crime is not an acceptable practice for civilized countries. The United States ratified the convention in 1955 without objecting to any of the guidelines. This means that if war broke out, juvenile offenders in countries occupied by the United States would not be subject to the death penalty. However, juvenile offenders in the United States could be.

Only the United States and a handful of other countries continue to execute juveniles or those who committed crimes while under the age of eighteen. According to Amnesty International, only eight countries in the world have executed juvenile offenders since 1986. These include Bangladesh, Iraq, Nigeria, Pakistan, Saudi Arabia, Yemen, and the United States. The majority were carried out in the United States.[2]

Except for the United States, the countries most commonly held up as examples of modern, civilized societies are all missing from the list. Critics say this only shows how far out of line the United States is on this issue.

The Death Penalty Discriminates

In the 1800s, two African Americans and one American Indian were convicted of killing a white man. They were tried, convicted, and executed. They were twelve years old.[3] Would this have happened if the children had been white? If the victim had been black? In 1964, James Echols, a black teenager, was executed in Texas for raping a white woman when he was seventeen. Would he have been executed for rape if his victim had been black?

In a system where justice is supposed to be colorblind, statistics show a different story. African-American young people make up 26 percent of arrests but 41 percent of those held in jail and 52 percent of those tried as adults.[4] In some cases, the difference is because more African-American juveniles are arrested for serious offenses, which carry stiffer penalties. However, Justice Department figures show that black juveniles often receive tougher sentences than whites for the same crimes.[5]

According to a study of all juveniles (whose race was recorded) executed since 1600, 69 percent were black and only 25 percent white. In the years after 1900, 75 percent were black. In addition, all forty-three juveniles who were executed for rape were African-American.[6]

Of the nine known cases of females executed for juvenile crimes, eight were African-American and the other was American Indian. Among juvenile offenders currently on death row, two thirds are minorities.[7] Steven Hawkins, executive director of the National Coalition to Abolish the Death Penalty, says, "What that tells me is that while we as a society are willing to give second chances to white children, that understanding gets lost when it comes to black or Latino kids."[8]

Juvenile Offenders Can Be Turned Around

Joseph Cannon was seventeen when he attempted to sexually assault a woman who had trusted him enough to let him stay in her home after he received probation for a burglary charge. He shot her seven

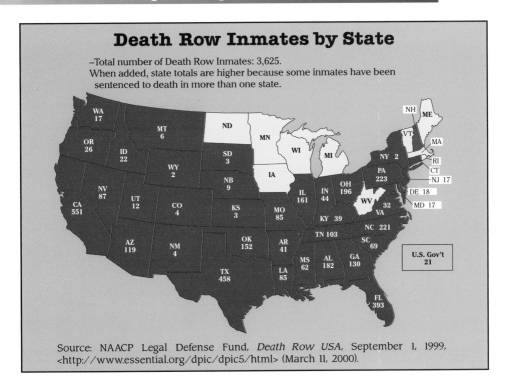

Death Row Inmates by State

–Total number of Death Row Inmates: 3,625.
When added, state totals are higher because some inmates have been sentenced to death in more than one state.

WA	17
MT	6
ND	
MN	
NH	
ME	
OR	26
ID	22
SD	3
WI	
MI	
VT	
MA	
NY	2
WY	2
IA	
PA	223
RI	
CT	
NB	9
IL	161
IN	44
OH	196
NJ	17
NV	87
UT	12
CO	4
KS	3
MO	85
WV	32
DE	18
MD	17
CA	551
KY	39
VA	
NC	221
AZ	119
NM	4
OK	152
AR	41
TN	103
SC	69
MS	62
AL	182
GA	130
U.S. Gov't	21
TX	458
LA	85
FL	393

Source: NAACP Legal Defense Fund, *Death Row USA*, September 1, 1999, <http://www.essential.org/dpic/dpic5/html> (March 11, 2000).

times, killing her. During the twenty-one years he spent in prison for his crimes, Cannon taught himself to read and write and grew from a child to an adult. "This is a 38-year-old man," Cannon said of himself, "not a 17-year-old child. I sort of have a different outlook on life than I did then." Cannon had had a childhood that included being run over by a truck, suffering sexual abuse, and attempting suicide. But he said he had become a different person while in prison and considered himself rehabilitated.[9] Had Joseph Cannon been rehabilitated? Would he be able to become a productive member of society? There is no way to know. He was executed April 22, 1998.

Critics say that the death penalty is a poor way to deal with troubled youths. Mark Soler, of the Youth Law Center in San Francisco, says the best plan would be to "take the most violent juveniles, lock them up for the protection of the community, and put lots of resources into working to rehabilitate them."[10]

A study of more than four hundred programs found those that provided counseling, education, and training in how to modify violent behavior reduced the number of those returning to crime by 40 percent. On the other hand, the study showed that boot camps, military-style programs that supposedly scare kids straight, actually produce a 10 to 12 percent increase in repeat offenders.[11] In 1999, there were more than fifty boot camps housing about four thousand five hundred juveniles. Studies for the Justice Department showed that 64 to 75 percent of the graduates went on to commit other crimes (about the same as traditional facilities). This has led states to look for better ways to treat young offenders.[12]

People who favor rehabilitation point to success stories such as Gina Grant. Gina was fourteen when she killed her mother by hitting her on the head with a candlestick. She served a few months in a juvenile facility and was on probation (special supervision) until she was eighteen. A bright student, she studied hard and was accepted for admission by Harvard University. But Harvard refused to admit her when they discovered she had been convicted of murder. Tufts University admitted her, however, saying she had paid her debt to society.

The Death Penalty Does Not Prevent Crime

Many young people cannot fully grasp the results of their actions. Death penalty critics say the death penalty does not act as a deterrent for them because they cannot fear something they do not understand. Teenagers often feel that nothing bad can happen to them. They may use drugs or alcohol, drive recklessly, or take part in other dangerous activities without concern for the consequences. This attitude, say critics, means that it is unlikely that teenagers will take the threat of capital punishment seriously. In fact, it may even make the idea of committing the crime more thrilling (the same way that antidrug messages sometimes make drugs seem more exciting).

Juvenile offenders can get used to being let off easy. Some may be convicted time and again, without ever spending time in prison. Then, they commit a crime and get charged as an adult and it is an entirely different situation. "Five times out of six," says Penn State professor Thomas Bernard, "you get away scot free. One time out of six, you get your brains blown out."[13]

Many juvenile homicides, particularly mass killings such as school shootings, seem to have a suicidal aspect to them. When two students stormed Columbine High School in Littleton, Colorado, in 1999 and killed twelve classmates and a teacher, they also killed themselves. Kip Kinkel, age fifteen, killed his parents and shot twenty-four students at his school in Springfield, Oregon, in 1998. When schoolmates wrestled him to the ground, he yelled "Shoot Me!" Death penalty critics say cases such as these show that some troubled kids may welcome death, not fear it. They are too disturbed to see the death penalty as a punishment.

Executing Teens Is Morally Wrong

*F*ifteen-year-old Kip Kinkel was charged with the murders of his parents and two high school students in 1998.

Some people think that it is not right to execute people who are not fully mature. Most violent juvenile offenders have had horrible childhoods. In fact, many were still in troubled homes when they committed the crime. Unlike adult offenders, who may have built a lifetime of violent behavior and are not likely to be rehabilitated, with help, juveniles may grow out of the effects of their childhoods. They might make something of their lives.

Because of their youth, juvenile offenders (particularly the youngest ones) are often unable to understand the effects of their actions. In 1998, a thirteen-year-old and an eleven-year-old killed four students and a teacher at their school in Jonesboro, Arkansas. Afterward, one of the boys involved expressed a wish to "take back" what he had done. This shows childish thinking. It is a sign that the boy had no real understanding that death is permanent.

Society, say death penalty critics, has a responsibility to protect its children—even those who are so troubled that they commit crimes.

Chapter 5

Human Rights and Constitutionality

In addition to the arguments over whether the death penalty helps prevent crime and whether it is morally right, there is also the issue of whether it is legal. This discussion centers on whether the United States Constitution allows the death penalty as a punishment and whether it is acceptable under international human rights law.

The United States in a Global Community

While the United States has been increasing the number of crimes eligible for the death penalty, reducing the rights of the defendant to appeal, and increasing the number and the speed of executions, other countries are moving away from the death penalty. Most countries have abolished the death penalty. All but a few have banned its use for juvenile offenders. The Council of Europe has made the elimination of the death penalty a condition of membership, considering it a sign of a mature society.

The United States imposes economic sanctions on countries that violate human rights. Suppose the other countries of the world were to impose sanctions on the United States for its use of the death penalty? How serious will the United States be taken on its stand for human rights while it is violating the human rights laws in several international agreements? As it is, some countries have refused to return escaped American criminals unless the United States agrees not to execute them.[1]

Executions Around the World

In 1998, there were 1,625 known executions in 37 countries, 80 percent of which took place in China, the Democratic Republic of Congo, the United States, and Iran. Because these figures include only documented cases, the true figures are likely to be much higher.

China **1,067**	Singapore **28**	Japan **6**	Lebanon **2**	Sudan **1**
Congo **100** (DR)	Sierra Leone **24**	Nigeria **6**	Bahamas **2**	Somalia **several**
USA **68**	Rwanda **24**	Oman **6**	Guatemala **1**	Iraq **?**
Iran **66**	Vietnam **18**	Cuba **5**	Ethiopia **1**	Saint Christopher & Nevis **?**
Egypt **48**	Yemen **17**	Kyrgyzstan **4**	Syria **1**	Uzbekistan **?**
Belarus **33**	Afghanistan **10**	Pakistan **4**	United Arab Emirates **1**	
Taiwan **32**	Jordan **9**	Zimbabwe **2**	Thailand **1**	
Saudi Arabia **29**	Kuwait **6**	Palestinian Authority **2**	Russian Federation **1**	

Hundreds of executions were reported in Iraq, although Amnesty International was unable to confirm most of the reports.

Source: Amnesty International, 1999, <http://www.essential.org/dpic/dpicintl.html> (March 11, 2000).

A few countries have increased their use of the death penalty, usually as a result of political unrest or changes in leadership. The Democratic Republic of Congo, for example, had only one execution in 1997. Then a new government came into power. In 1999, a United Nations official reported that the new president's Military Court of Order had ordered the execution of 250 people during 1998 and 1999.[2] Many of those executed were civilians who actively opposed the government, or soldiers found guilty of military offenses such as helping the enemy. One death sentence was successfully appealed, that of a fifteen-year-old soldier.[3]

Capital Punishment As a Human Rights Issue

Three international treaties were created to encourage countries to get rid of their death penalties. These treaties are the Sixth Protocol to the European Convention on Human Rights, the Second Optional Protocol to the International Covenant on Civil and Political Rights, and the Protocol to the American Convention on Human Rights to Abolish the Death Penalty. In addition, both the International Covenant on Human Rights and the United Nations Convention on the Rights of the Child forbid executing someone who was under the age of eighteen at the time of the crime. More than one hundred countries have either signed one of these treaties or have laws that forbid the execution of juvenile offenders.[4]

Nearly all the countries of the world signed the International Covenant on Civil and Political Rights, which went into effect in 1976. This treaty includes a section that says, "Sentence of death shall not be imposed for crimes committed by persons below eighteen years of age . . . " Even though the United States signed the treaty in 1977 and ratified (officially approved) it in 1992, it reserved the right to treat children as adults "in exceptional circumstances." This included what they claimed was their right to imprison children with adults and to execute juvenile offenders. The United States is also one of the few countries to fail to ratify the Convention on the Rights of the Child, which also forbids executing juvenile offenders.[5]

In April 1999, the United Nations Human Rights Commission passed a resolution calling for a worldwide halt on executions. Voting against the resolution were ten countries, including China, Pakistan, Rwanda, Sudan, and the United States. The resolution specifically called on countries to stop giving the death penalty to juvenile offenders.[6]

One of the reasons the United States does not go along with international treaties is that death penalty laws are made by individual states. Texas and Virginia, for example, perform many executions, while Massachusetts, Michigan, the District of Columbia, and ten other states do not have a death penalty. The United Nations Special Rapporteur (someone who brings back information) wrote in his 1998 report on the United States that there is a gap between what the federal government does and what the states do. While the United States government might sign an international agreement, individual states make up their own rules.[7]

When states try to determine what is legal as far as the death penalty, particularly when it comes to juvenile offenders, they tend to look to other states for guidance, not to world opinion or international law. For example, when deciding the case of

Michael Domingues, a sixteen-year-old convicted of killing a neighbor and her child, the Nevada Supreme Court considered that other states had laws allowing the death penalty for offenders under the age of eighteen. Those laws had been challenged in the Supreme Court and allowed to stand. The Nevada court used this fact to justify giving Domingues the death penalty.[8]

Some death row inmates have used international law to try to stop their executions. Douglas Christopher Thomas appealed to the Supreme Court based on the fact that the International Covenant on Civil and Political Rights prohibits the execution of juvenile offenders. The Court refused to hear his appeal and he was executed January 10, 2000. The Court also refused to consider Michael Domingues's case, which was appealed for the same reason.

The Death Penalty and the Law

In 1972, the U.S. Supreme Court ruled that the death penalty—as it was being used—was a cruel and unusual punishment. The Court said that states were not following any consistent guidelines. This ruling, *Georgia* v. *Furman*, outlawed the death penalty and reversed death sentences that had already been given. It did not say that the death penalty was unconstitutional, only that it had not been used properly. The Court forbade its use until states could create better laws governing its use.

In 1976, the Court lifted the death penalty ban in a decision known as *Gregg* v. *Georgia*. The states of Florida, Georgia, and Texas had created new laws that gave juries and judges guidelines to help them determine whether the death penalty should be given. These three cases were combined under the

*D*eath penalty protestors staged a mock execution at the U.S. Supreme Court building in Washington, D.C., on July 1, 1996. The date marked the twentieth anniversary of the court's decision to reinstate the death penalty.

Gregg ruling, which approved the laws and said that the death penalty was constitutional. Since that time, thirty-eight states and the federal government have enacted death penalty laws similar to the ones the Court upheld in the *Gregg* decision. The decision also introduced the idea that judges and juries could consider aggravating circumstances (such as extreme cruelty), which would call for a stronger sentence, or mitigating circumstances (such as the age of the offender), which would call for a lesser sentence.

A case that directly affected juvenile offenders

was *Thompson* v. *Oklahoma* in 1988. This case decided that, according to the Constitution, defendants under the age of sixteen at the time of the offense could not be executed. Then, in 1989, *Stanford* v. *Kentucky* determined that it was constitutional to execute offenders who were at least sixteen at the time of the crime. (States can set their own age limits above sixteen.) *Thompson* is widely understood to prohibit execution of offenders who committed crimes when under the age of sixteen even though states have set their own minimums and some have no minimum age at all.[9]

State governments are not the only ones to have death penalty laws. The United States government also has a death penalty, which is used for federal offenses such as treason (betraying the country). In 1994, the federal death penalty was expanded under a broad crime bill to include about forty different offenses. Some of the crimes for which the federal death penalty was authorized include: kidnappings resulting in death, drive-by shootings, and running large-scale drug operations. Although the last federal execution was in 1963 (other executions are by individual states), many people have been sentenced to death in federal cases. Most of them are in prison waiting to appeal their sentences. Since the 1994 law, at least fifteen people have been given the federal death penalty, including Timothy J. McVeigh, who was convicted in the bombing of the Federal Building in Oklahoma City in 1995.[10]

During the 1980s, the Supreme Court was asked to determine the constitutionality of the death penalty for juveniles. In 1982, the Court overturned the death sentence in the case of Monty Lee Eddings, who had been sentenced to death for killing a highway patrol officer. He was sixteen at the time of the crime. The Court did not rule on whether the death penalty was cruel and unusual when applied to juveniles but decided that the lower court had failed to consider the mitigating factors. These included Eddings's history of emotional disturbance, the fact that he had been beaten by his father, and his bad family environment. These factors, combined with his age, according to the Court, should have been considered because he might have received a lesser sentence.[11] Justice Powell, writing for the majority, said, "Just as the chronological age of a minor is itself a relevant mitigating factor of great weight, so must the background and mental and emotional development of a youthful defendant be duly considered in sentencing."[12]

Chapter 6

Creating a Better System

After the Littleton school shootings in 1999, Congress tried to come up with a solution that would prevent future tragedies. Some argued for increased punishment such as creating minimum sentences for young people who commit crimes with guns. Others wanted stricter control over gun sales. Senators and congressional representatives discussed everything from making it illegal to expose children to violent movies, books, and video games to allowing schools to hang a copy of the Ten Commandments in classrooms. But it is much easier to look for someone to blame than to come up with solutions that will work.

Prevention Programs

Most people would agree that it is better to prevent crime than be forced to deal with its effects through means such as the death penalty. Experts say that putting more police officers on the street, reducing access to guns, counseling people with addiction problems, helping people find jobs, and stopping abuse will reduce crime. Providing mental health care and treatment to those who need it may also help.

*S*eventeen-year-old Lisandra Torres listens during a biology class at the Hartford Youthful Offender Program in Hartford, Connecticut. Torres, a former heroin addict, said that without the program she would have ended up back on the street or in prison for the rest of her life.

Some people have suggested punishing the parents of juvenile offenders. According to the National Conference of State Legislatures, forty-two states have laws that make parents responsible in some way for crimes committed by their children. Seventeen states make the parents criminally liable (they may have to pay large fines or even serve time in jail).[1] Child Access Prevention laws hold adults responsible when they allow guns to fall into the hands of juveniles. According to a study published in the *Journal of the American Medical Association*, accidental shooting deaths among children under age fifteen dropped by 23 percent in states covered by such laws.[2]

Many experts think access to guns is a large part of the problem of juvenile crime. While youth killings with other weapons neither increased nor decreased during the late 1980s, killings with guns skyrocketed. Handgun control advocates say that 43 percent of homes with children under age seventeen contain guns.[3]

Others say lack of supervision is to blame. Most juvenile crime occurs in the hours after school, when many kids have nothing to do and no one to watch them. Community center activities and after-school programs may help keep kids busy and supervised.

Alternative Sentencing

One alternative to the death penalty is already being used: life imprisonment without parole. Although some people think that most, if not all, criminals get out of prison after serving only a few years of their sentence, this is not the case. Nearly all states have a life sentence in which there is no possibility of parole for at least twenty-five years. Life with no parole means the person stays in prison until the day he or she dies.

Death penalty supporters say that life without parole is not a perfect solution. They point to cases in which sentencing laws were changed and offenders sentenced to life without parole became eligible for parole. Prisoners may also murder fellow inmates while in prison. In addition, in rare cases, prisoners can escape and murder more people.

Juvenile prisoners housed in adult prisons are at increased risk for injury. In 1998, Amnesty International issued a report that said that children were much more likely to be sexually or physically assaulted by staff members as well as inmates while in adult prisons than in juvenile facilities. William F. Schulz, executive director of Amnesty International USA, said, "Nothing is guaranteed to turn a confused, angry teenager into a bitter adult than abusing them when they are in prison, ignoring their mental health concerns and housing them with adults."[4] Thirty-eight states house juveniles in adult prisons with no special programs or educational services.

Rehabilitation

Most prisoners had difficult lives long before they got into trouble with the law. Their family backgrounds tend to contain poverty, absent or abusive parents, addiction problems, mental illness or low mental ability, and other problems. Do miserable child-hoods produce "bad seeds" that cannot be saved? Or can these kids be redirected, rehabilitated, and returned to society?

Most experts agree that the current juvenile justice system provides little opportunity for rehabilitation. Juvenile facilities are generally overcrowded and provide few, if any, educational or counseling programs. "We're creating monsters by putting [juveniles] into some of these things," observed Marion Mattingly, who conducted a Justice Department study of juvenile services in Washington, D.C.[5]

Programs that do try to rehabilitate juvenile offenders vary state to state and facility to facility. The Capital Offender Program at Giddings State Home and School in Giddings, Texas, uses intense therapy sessions as one tool. Offenders have to recreate the crime they committed to help them realize the seriousness of their actions. This includes imagining what the victim felt like while being stabbed or shot. Graduates of the program are 53 percent less likely to be arrested for a violent crime within a year of release than those with no treat-ment. The Youthful Offender Program at Madison Correctional Institution in Madison, Ohio, works with inmates to teach them to read, manage anger, handle drug or alcohol problems, and build their self-esteem.[6] These and other programs try to return juvenile offenders to society safely.

Number of Persons Executed in the United States, 1930–1999

Year	Number of Executions	Year	Number of Executions	Year	Number of Executions
1930	155	1954	81	1978	0
1931	153	1955	76	1979	2
1932	140	1956	65	1980	0
1933	160	1957	65	1981	1
1934	168	1958	49	1982	2
1935	199	1959	49	1983	5
1936	195	1960	56	1984	21
1937	147	1961	42	1985	18
1938	190	1962	47	1986	18
1939	160	1963	21	1987	25
1940	124	1964	15	1988	11
1941	123	1965	7	1989	16
1942	147	1966	1	1990	23
1943	131	1967	2	1991	14
1944	120	1968	0	1992	31
1945	117	1969	0	1993	27
1946	131	1970	0	1994	31
1947	153	1971	0	1995	56
1948	119	1972	0	1996	45
1949	119	1973	0	1997	74
1950	82	1974	0	1998	68
1951	105	1975	0	1999	98
1952	83	1976	0		
1953	62	1977	0		

"Capital Punishment, 1998," NCJ-179012, December 1999, <http://www.ojp.usdoj.gov/bjs/glance/exe.txt> (March 11, 2000).

Most experts agree that unless the system is improved, juvenile violent crime will continue. Federal juvenile justice chief John Wilson says that unless rehabilitation is offered, the United States can not claim that "the children have had an opportunity and they have failed." Instead, the nation will have to consider that "we have failed them."[7]

Applying the Death Penalty Fairly and Consistently

When sports star O.J. Simpson was found innocent of killing his wife, Nicole, and her friend Ron Goldman in a criminal trial, many people were shocked. They felt that the evidence was overwhelming that he was guilty. Some people believe that Simpson bought his freedom with expensive lawyers.

Poor defendants may not be able to afford a lawyer at all. For them, the court provides public defenders. Public defenders, however, are often overworked, underpaid, and have more experience with drug or theft cases than with complicated murder cases. That is one reason, say critics, poor people are more likely to get the death penalty.

Some say fairness problems would be solved by always giving the death penalty for certain crimes. Those crimes would be punished by death. Period. There would be no mitigating circumstances to reduce the sentence and no room for bargaining. Critics say that not being able to afford experienced legal counsel and prejudice on the part of the judge or jury would still mean that more minorities would be convicted (and therefore get the death penalty). They also say that such a system would prevent judges and juries from using their own judgment when deciding on a penalty.

One aspect of the death penalty that makes it both less effective in preventing crime and more cruel to the offender is the length of time it takes to be carried out. In 1999, Judge Reginald Stanton gave a death sentence to Thomas J. Koskovich for his role in the ambush and murder of two pizza delivery men. The New Jersey Superior Court judge added an unusual twist. He set a time limit on the execution. If the state does not execute Koskovich by May 7, 2004, the sentence will automatically change to life in prison. Judge Stanton said,

> The process has become unacceptably cruel to defendants, who spend long years under sentence of death while the judicial system conducts seemingly interminable [endless] proceedings which remind many observers of a cruelly whimsical cat toying with a mouse.[8]

Stop Executions Until Fairness Problems Are Solved

Some people feel that all executions should be halted until some of the issues are sorted out. They are concerned that the death penalty may be discriminatory, that it may not prevent crime, and that it may cause innocent people to be executed. Critics are particularly worried about the treatment of teenage offenders.

According to researchers who studied juveniles on death row during the 1980s,

> Juveniles accused of a capital offense are uniquely vulnerable; they lack the maturity or insight to recognize the importance of psychiatric or neurological symptoms to their defense; and they

are dependent on family for assistance in a way that adult offenders are not.[9]

Unfortunately, many of these offenders come from terrible home situations. It is unlikely that they have adults in their lives who are willing and able to help them.

On April 26, 2000, U. S. Senator Russ Feingold introduced the Death Penalty Moratorium Bill. The Bill called for the federal government and all states that have a death penalty to suspend (temporarily stop) executions. A commission would then review current death penalty practices and make recommendations for fixing the system's flaws. Executions would resume only if the commission determined that the death penalty would be used fairly and appropriately. The Bill would have to be passed by Congress to become law.

Death penalty opponents say capital punishment is a cruel and unusual punishment that is applied unfairly. They point to the overwhelming number of nations around the world that have eliminated the death penalty or at least stopped executing juvenile offenders. People who support the death penalty say it is a way to reduce crime and stop violent criminals. The vicious nature of some crimes, they say, justifies execution as an effective, fair punishment. They argue that victims' families deserve to see justice in the form of the death penalty regardless of the murderer's age. Perhaps there are alternatives such as life without parole or high-security rehabilitation programs that might protect society while assuring that the United States is upholding worldwide human rights standards. As executions continue to take place in America, the death penalty debate will go on.

Amnesty International
322 Eighth Ave.
New York, NY 10001
(212) 807-8400
<http://www.amnesty.org>

Citizens Against Homicide
P.O. Box 2115
San Anselmo, CA 94979
(415) 455-5944
<http://www.murdervictims.com/cah.htm>

Death Penalty Education Center
12651 Briar Forest
Suite 153
Houston, TX 77077
(281) 493-6232

Death Penalty Information Center
1320 18th St., N.W., 5th Floor
Washington, DC 20036
(202) 293-6970
<http://www.essential.org/dpic>

Justice for All
P.O. Box 55159
Houston, TX 77255
(713) 935-9300
<http://www.jfa.net>

National Coalition to Abolish the Death Penalty
1436 U St., N.W.
Suite 104
Washington, DC 20009
(888) 286-2237
<http://www.ncadp.org>

Chapter 1.   Brief History of the Death Penalty

1. University of Alaska Anchorage Justice Center Web Site, "Focus on the Death Penalty: History and Recent Developments," n.d., <http://www.uaa.alaska.edu/just/death/history.html> (January 24, 2000).

2. Ibid.

3. Death Penalty Information Center Web Site, "Executions by Region of the Country," n.d., <http://www.essential.org/dpic/dpicreg.html> (January 24, 2000).

4. Death Penalty Information Center Web Site, "Executions by Method Used," n.d., <http://www.essential.org/dpic/dpicexec.html> (January 24, 2000).

5. Death Penalty Information Center Web Site, "The Death Penalty in 1999: Year End Report," December, 1999, <http://www.essential.org/dpic/yrendrpt99.html> (January 24, 2000).

6. Death Penalty Information Center, "The Death Penalty: An International Perspective," n.d., <http://www.essential.org/dpic/dpicintl.html> (January 28, 2000).

7. Death Penalty Information Center, "What's New: Last Updated April 29, 1999," <http://www.essential.org> (May 3, 1999), p. 4.

8. Margaret Jasper, *The Law of Capital Punishment*, Oceana's Legal Almanac Series: Law for the Layperson (Dobbs Ferry, N.Y.: Oceana Publications, 1998), p. 22.

9. Martha Brant, "Last Chance Class," *Newsweek*, May 31, 1999, p. 34.

10. Death Penalty Information Center, "The Death Penalty in 1998: Year End Report," December 1998, <http://www.essential.org/dpic/yrendrpt98.html> (January 24, 2000), p. 3.

11. Ibid., p. 2.

12. Jasper, p. 31.

13. Ibid., p. 33.

14. Michael L. Radelet, "Post-Furman Botched Executions," Death Penalty Information Center, n.d., <http://www.essential.org/dpic/botched.html> (May 22, 1999).

15. ABCNEWS.com, "Split Decision on Death Penalty," January 19, 2000, <http://abcnews.go.com/sections/politics/DailyNews/poll000119.html> (January 28, 2000).

16. Christopher John Farley and James Willwerth, "The Kids on the Row," *Time*, January 19, 1998, vol. 151, no. 2, Time.com, <http://cgi.pathfinder.com/time/magazine/1998/dom/980119/crime.a_time_investigati5.html> (May 19, 1999), p. 2.

Chapter 2. Executing Teens

1. Shirley Dicks, ed., "Juveniles on Death Row: Case Profiles," *Young Blood: Juvenile Justice and the Death Penalty* (Amherst, N.Y.: Prometheus Books, 1995), pp. 150, 151.

2. Amnesty International, "USA Violating International Law: Child Offender Executed, Two More Scheduled to Die," n.d. <http://www.amnesty.ca/library/news/amr510400.htm> (May 4, 2000).

3. Death Penalty Information Center, "What's New: Last Updated April 29, 1999," <http://www.essential.org> (May 3, 1999), p. 6.

4. Death Penalty Information Center, "Executions of Juvenile Offenders," n.d., <http://www.essential.org/dpic/juvexec.html> (May 4, 2000), p. 2.

5. Amnesty International, "Pakistan: Placing Children on Death Row—'In the Best Interests of the Child?'" May 22,1999, <http://www.amnestyusa.org/news/1999/33301299.htm> (May 4, 2000)

6. National Coalition Against the Death Penalty, "Death Row Kids," n.d., <http://www.ncadp.org/drkids.html> (May 6, 1999), p. 2; Charlene Hall, "Justice for All," personal communication, May 19, 1999.

7. Patricia Edmonds, "To Some, Ultimate Penalty is Ageless," *USA Today*, September 28, 1994, p. 11.

8. Death Penalty Information Center, "Juveniles and the Death Penalty," n.d., <http://www.essential.org/juvchar.html> (May 3, 1999), pp. 1–2.

Chapter 3. Arguments for the Death Penalty for Teens

1. Death Penalty Information Center, "Juveniles and the Death Penalty," n.d., <http://www.essential.org/juvchar.html> (May 3, 1999), p. 1.

2. United States Department of Justice, "Homicide Trends in the United States," n.d., <http://www.ojp.usdoj.gov/bjs/abstract/htius.htm> (May 4, 2000), p. 1.

3. Thomas A. Vonder Haar, "A Free Ride for Juvenile Offenders," *St. Louis Post-Dispatch*, May 2, 1995, p. 13B.

4. Patricia Edmonds and Sam Vincent Meddis, "Crime & Punishment: Is Juvenile Justice System Creating Monsters?: Public Angry Over Level of Violence," *USA Today*, September 28, 1994, p. 1.

5. Charlotte Faltermayer, "What Is Justice for a Sixth-Grade Killer?" *Time*, April 6, 1998, vol. 151, no. 13, Time.com, <http://cgi.pathfinder.com/time/magazine/1998/dom/980406/box1.html> (May 19, 1999), p. 1.

6. Christopher John Farley and James Willwerth, "The Kids on the Row," *Time*, January 19, 1998, vol. 151, no. 2, Time.com, <http://cgi.pathfinder.com/time/magazine/1998/dom/980119/crime.a_time_investigati5.html> (May 19, 1999), p. 2.

7. Edmonds and Meddis, p. 1.

8. Ladale Lloyd, "Victim's Father Testifies for the Death Penalty," *The Tampa Tribune*, June 17, 1999, p. 1.

9. Randy Boddie, personal communication, June 20, 1999.

Chapter 4. Arguments Against the Death Penalty for Teens

1. Amnesty International USA, "On the Wrong Side of History: Children and the Death Penalty in the USA," n.d., <http://www.amnesty.it/ailib/aipub/1998/amr/25105898.htm> (May 4, 2000), p. 4.

2. Margaret Jasper, *The Law of Capital Punishment*, Oceana's Legal Almanac Series: Law for the Layperson (Dobbs Ferry, N.Y.: Oceana Publications, 1998), p. 38.

3. Shirley Dicks, ed., "Juveniles on Death Row: Case Profiles," *Young Blood: Juvenile Justice and the Death Penalty* (Amherst, N.Y.: Prometheus Books, 1995), p. 151.

4. Paul Wellstone and David Cole, "Balance Check: We Need to Track the Jailing of Young Minorities," *The Washington Post*, June 14, 1999, p. A21.

5. Ibid., p. 34.

6. Dicks, p. 152.

7. Death Penalty Information Center, "Juveniles and the Death Penalty," n.d., <http://www.essential.org/juvchar.html> (May 3, 1999), p. 1.

8. Christopher John Farley and James Willwerth, "Dead Teen Walking," *Time*, January 19, 1998, vol. 151, no. 2, Time.com, <http://cgi.pathfinder.com/time/magazine/1998/dom/980119/crime.a_time_investigati6.html> (May 19, 1999), p. 1.

9. Charisse Jones, "Old Enough to Pay the Ultimate Penalty," *USA Today*, April 13, 1998, p. 10A.

10. Patricia Edmonds and Sam Vincent Meddis, "Crime & Punishment: Is Juvenile Justice System Creating Monsters?: Public Angry Over Level of Violence," *USA Today*, September 28, 1994, p. 1.

11. Ibid.

12. Alexandra Marks, "States Fall Out of (Tough) Love with Boot Camps," *The Christian Science Monitor*, December 27, 1999, p. 3.

13. Edmonds and Meddis, p. 1.

Chapter 5. Human Rights and Constitutionality

1. Patricia Edmonds and Sam Vincent Meddis, "Crime & Punishment: Is Juvenile Justice System Creating Monsters?: Public Angry Over Level of Violence," *USA Today*, September 28, 1994, p. 1.

2. Associated Press, "U.N.: Congo Ordered 250 Executed," AP Online, August 23, 1999.

3. Amnesty International, "Scores of Executions in the Democratic Republic of Congo," M2 PressWIRE, n.d., <http://www.amnestyusa.org/news/1999/16201599.htm> (May 4, 2000).

4. Margaret Jasper, *The Law of Capital Punishment*, Oceana's Legal Almanac Series: Law for the Layperson (Dobbs Ferry, N.Y.: Oceana Publications, 1998), p. 38.

5. Death Penalty Information Center, "What's New: Last Updated April 29, 1999," <http://www.essential.org> (May 3, 1999), p. 6.

6. Ibid., p.1.

7. Amnesty International USA, "On the Wrong Side of History: Children and the Death Penalty in the USA," n.d., <http://www.amnesty.it/ailib/aipub/1998/amr/25105898.htm> (May 4, 2000), p. 3.

8. Ibid.

9. Victor Streib, "Minimum Death Penalty Ages by American Jurisdiction," n.d., <http://www.essential.org/dpic/juvagelim.html> (June 29, 1998), p. 1.

10. Linda Greenhouse, "Examining the Death Penalty Law," *The New York Times*, February 23, 1999, p. A18.

11. Shirley Dicks, ed., "Juveniles on Death Row: Case Profiles," *Young Blood: Juvenile Justice and the Death Penalty* (Amherst, N.Y.: Prometheus Books, 1995), p. 153.

12. Ibid., p. 154.

Chapter 6. Creating a Better System

1. Charlotte Faltermayer, "What Is Justice for a Sixth-Grade Killer?" *Time*, April 6, 1998, vol. 151, no. 13, Time.com, <http://cgi.pathfinder.com/time/magazine/1998/dom/980406/box1.html>, p. 2.

2. Ibid., p. 3.

3. Jeffrey Obser, "Child's Play Turns Deadly," *Newsday*, March 15, 1999, p. A13.

4. National News Briefs, "Rights Group Criticizes United States on Jailing Youths," *The New York Times*, November 18, 1998, p. A28.

5. Patricia Edmonds and Sam Vincent Meddis, "Crime & Punishment: Is Juvenile Justice System Creating Monsters?: Public Angry Over Level of Violence," *USA Today*, September 28, 1994, p. 1.

6. Karen S. Peterson. "Public Clamors: Get Tough at a Tender Age," *USA Today*, September 29, 1998, p. 10D.

7. Edmonds and Meddis, p. 1.

8. Robert Hanley, "Judge Orders Death Penalty With a 5-Year Deadline," *The New York Times*, May 8, 1999, p. B5.

9. Shirley Dicks, ed., "Juveniles on Death Row: Case Profiles," *Young Blood: Juvenile Justice and the Death Penalty* (Amherst, N.Y.: Prometheus Books, 1995), p. 157.

Barbour, Scott. *Teen Violence*. San Diego: Greenhaven Press, 1999.

Cox, Vic. *Guns, Violence & Teens*. Hillside, N.J.: Enslow Publishers, 1997.

Flaherty, Sara, and Austin Sarat. *Victims and Victims' Rights*. New York: Chelsea House Publishers, 1998.

Grabowski, John. *The Death Penalty*. San Diego: Lucent Books, 1998.

Jones, Delores. *Race, Crime and Punishment*. New York: Chelsea House Publishers, 1998.

Kim, Henny H., ed. *Guns and Violence*. San Diego: Greenhaven Press, 1999.

Netzley, Patricia. *Issues in Crime*. San Diego: Lucent Books, 2000.

Winters, Paul A., ed. *The Death Penalty: Opposing Viewpoints*. San Diego: Greenhaven Press, 1997.

Further Reading

Index